WHALES

GRAY WHALES

JOHN F. PREVOST
ABDO & Daughters

Published by Abdo & Daughters, 4940 Viking Drive, Suite 622, Edina, Minnesota 55435.

Library bound edition distributed by Rockbottom Books, Pentagon Tower, P.O. Box 36036, Minneapolis, Minnesota 55435.

Printed in the United States.

Cover Photo credit: Peter Arnold, Inc.

Interior Photo credits: Peter Arnold, Inc.

Edited by Bob Italia

Library of Congress Cataloging-in-Publication Data

Prevost, John F.
   Gray whales / John F. Prevost.
     p. cm. — (Whales)
   Includes bibliographical references (p. 23) and index.
   ISBN 1-56239-476-2
1. Gray whale—Juvenile literature. [1. Gray whale. 2. Whales.] I. Title. II.
Series Prevost, John F. Whales.
  QL737.C425P74 1995
   599.5'1—dc20

                    95-9677
                       CIP
                       AC

ABOUT THE AUTHOR
John Prevost is a marine biologist and diver who has been active in conservation and education issues for the past 18 years. Currently he is living inland and remains actively involved in freshwater and marine husbandry, conservation and education projects.

Contents

GRAY WHALES AND FAMILY 4

SIZE, SHAPE AND COLOR....................... 6

WHERE THEY LIVE 8

SENSES 10

DEFENSE..................................... 12

FOOD 14

BABIES 16

GRAY WHALE FACTS 18

GLOSSARY 20

INDEX 22

BIBLIOGRAPHY 23

GRAY WHALES AND FAMILY

Gray whales are **mammals** that live in the sea. Like humans, they are **warm blooded**, breathe air with lungs, and **nurse** their young with milk. They are called gray whales because of their spotted gray skin color.

There use to be 3 different gray whale groups. The North Atlantic whales were wiped out. The Northwest Pacific whales, hunted until 1966, are almost gone. The Northeast Pacific (Californian) gray whales, once heavily hunted, are now protected by law and are making a comeback.

Cousins to the gray whale are the humpback whale, blue whale, and minke whale.

Gray whales get their name from their spotted gray skin color.

SIZE, SHAPE AND COLOR

Gray whales may reach a length of 47 to 50 feet (14.3 to 15.2 meters). Females are slightly larger than males.

Gray whales are thick bodied and have a slim, triangle-shaped head. A row of bumps on their back replaces the **dorsal** fin. Their entire body, **flippers** and **flukes** are a spotted gray. The skin along the top of the head and back is often covered with patches of white, yellow, or orange **barnacles**.

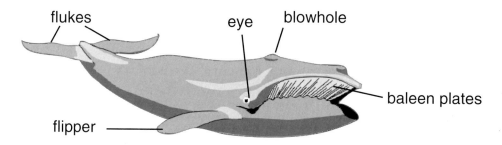

Baleen whales share the same features.

Gray whales have triangle-shaped heads with patches of white, yellow, or orange barnacles on their skin.

Gray whales are called **baleen** whales because they have baleen plates instead of teeth.

WHERE THEY LIVE

Gray whales were once found in the North Atlantic and North Pacific. The only gray whales left are in the North Pacific. There are 2 North Pacific groups: Northeast (Californian) group and the Northwest group.

The Northeast (Californian) group **migrates** 7,000 miles (11,265 kilometers) each year from the Arctic and Bering seas to Baja California and Mexico.

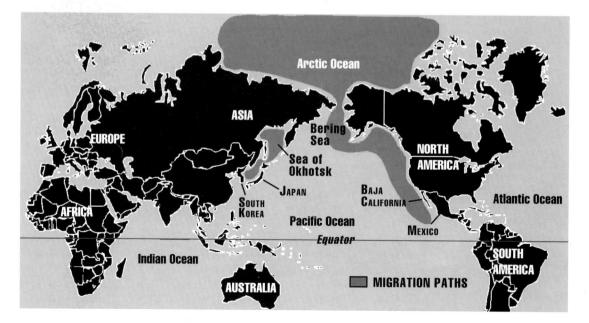

Gray whale rescue near Barrow, Alaska.

The rare Northwest group **migrates** from the Sea of Okhotsk, north of Japan, to the South Korean coast.

Most **baleen** whales live in deep water. But gray whales like water no deeper than 820 feet (250 meters).

SENSES

Gray whales and people have 4 of the same senses. Their eyesight is good in and out of the water. If they wish to see above the water, they raise their head above the surface.

Hearing is their best sense. Gray whales are **social** animals. They will use **echolocation** to **communicate** with each other and to find food. Their loud grunts, groans, and bubble-burst sounds can be heard for over 1.2 miles (2 kilometers). Because it is thick, water passes on sound better than air.

HOW ECHOLOCATION WORKS

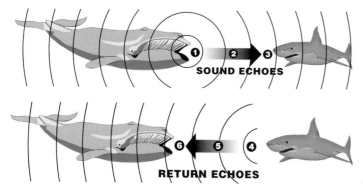

SOUND ECHOES

RETURN ECHOES

The whale sends out sound echoes (1). These echoes travel in all directions through the water (2). The sound echoes reach an object in the whale's path (3), then bounce off it (4). The return echoes travel through the water (5) and reach the whale (6). These echoes let the whale know where the object is, how large it is, and how fast it is moving.

The eye of a gray whale.

Touch is also an important sense. Tiny hairs around the upper jaw are used during feeding. These hairs improve the sense of touch. Gray whales have the sense of taste but do not have the sense of smell.

DEFENSE

Killer whales and large sharks **prey** on gray whales. Female gray whales will protect their **calves** from **predators** using their size and weight. Small boats have been damaged by female gray whales protecting their calves.

Man has been the leading predator of gray whales for the last 300 years. But hunting laws protect the Northeast Pacific (Californian) gray whales.

*Hunting laws protect gray whales
so people can enjoy them.*

FOOD

Gray whales do not have any teeth. Instead, they have 130 to 180 small **baleen** plates on each side of the upper jaw. The plates bend and are trimmed with bristles.

Gray whales feed by sucking water, mud or **kelp** into their large throats. As the water is squeezed out, **prey** is trapped in bristles on the baleen plates. Gray whales eat worms, small shellfish, and small fish.

A young gray whale showing its baleen plates.

BABIES

A baby gray whale is called a **calf.** A newborn calf is 15 to 16.5 feet (4.6 to 5 meters) long and is gray. As it grows older, the gray color becomes spotted.

A calf needs its mother for safety and food. Since whales are **mammals**, the young will **nurse** for up to 9 months. The young whale will not become an adult until it is 8 to 12 years old.

Californian gray whales, mother and calf.

GRAY WHALE FACTS

Scientific Name: *Eschrichtius robustus*

Average Size: 47 to 50 feet (14.3 to 15.2 meters)
Females are slightly larger than
males.

Where They're Found:

- •Northwest Pacific gray whales,
 nearly gone.
- •Northeast Pacific (Californian) gray
 whales follow **migration** paths
 between polar and tropical waters.

The tail of a gray whale off the Baja California coast.

GLOSSARY

BALEEN (buh-LEEN) - A hard flexible material growing in place of teeth and attached to the upper jaw; also called whalebone.

BARNACLE (BAR-na-kull) - A shellfish (relative of the crab, lobster and shrimp) which attaches to shipbottoms, pilings, and whales.

CALF - A baby whale.

COMMUNICATE (huk-MEW-nih-kate) - To exchange feelings, thoughts, or information.

DORSAL (DOOR-sull) - Of, on, or near the back.

ECHOLOCATION (ek-oh-low-KAY-shun) - The use of sound waves to find objects.

FLIPPERS - The forelimbs of a sea mammal.

FLUKE - One of the two lobes of a whale's tail.

KELP - Brown seaweed growing along the coasts of the Atlantic and Pacific oceans.

MAMMAL - A class of animals, including humans, that have hair and feed their young milk.

MIGRATION (my-GRAY-shun) - To travel from one region to another in search of food or to reproduce.

NURSE - To feed a young animal milk from the mother's breasts.

PREDATOR (PRED-uh-ter) - An animal that eats other animals.

PREY - Animals that are eaten by other animals.

SOCIAL (SOE-shull) - Living in organized groups.

WARM-BLOODED - An animal whose body temperature remains the same and warmer than the outside air or water temperature.

Index

A

air 10
Arctic 8

B

babies 16
back 6
Baja California 8
baleen plates 7, 14
baleen whale 7
barnacles 6
Bering Sea 8
blue whale 4
breathe 4
bristles 14

C

calf 12, 16
color 4, 6, 16
communication 10

D

defense 12
dorsal fin 6

E

echolocation 10
eyesight 10

F

family 4
feeding 11
fish 14
flippers 6
fluke 6
food 14, 16

G

gray whale facts 18
gray whale, female 6, 12
gray whale, male 6

H

hairs 11
head 6, 10
hearing 10
humpback whale 4
hunting 4

J

Japan 9
jaw 11, 14

K

kelp 14
killer whales 12

L

law 4, 12
length 6
lungs 4

M

mammals 4, 16
Mexico 8
migration 8, 9, 18
minke whale 4
mud 14

N

North Atlantic group
    4, 8

North Pacific groups 8
Northeast Pacific
    (Californian) group
    4, 8, 12, 18
Northwest Pacific group 4,
    8, 9, 18
nurse 4, 16

P

predator 12
prey 12, 14

S

Sea of Okhotsk 9
senses 10
shape 6
sharks 12
size 6, 12, 16, 18
skin 4
smell 11
social animal 10
South Korea 9
spots 4, 6, 16

T

taste 11
teeth 7, 14
throat 14
touch 11

W

water 10, 14
weight 12
worms 14

BIBLIOGRAPHY

Cousteau, Jacques-Yves. *The Whale, Mighty Monarch of the Sea*. N.Y.: Doubleday, 1972.

Dozier, Thomas A. *Whales and Other Sea Mammals*. Time-Life Films, 1977.

Leatherwood, Stephen. *The Sierra Club Handbook of Whales and Dolphins*. San Francisco, California: Sierra Club Books, 1983.

Minasian, Stanley M. *The World's Whales*. Washington, D.C.: Smithsonian Books, 1984.

Ridgway, Sam H., ed. *Mammals of the Sea*. Springfield, Illinois: Charles C. Thomas Publisher, 1972.